This Journal Belongs To:

_____

"Have patience with all things - but first with yourself. Never confuse your mistakes with your value as a human being. You are perfectly valuable, creative, worthwhile person simply because you exist. And no amount of triumphs or tribulations can ever change that."

-Saint Francis de Sales

A Note from the Authors

We created this journal specifically for Catholic women in mind. **My Catholic Planners and Journals** was founded by a Catholic couple with six kids. So, we understand how chaotic life can be and the need to remember the positives.

We took our faith for granted early in our marriage and are now grateful that God has given us the grace to embrace it.

With all of the daily struggles that come with raising a family, it is easy to forget all of the blessings we have in our lives. The stresses of work, educating the kids, sickness, financial issues, miscarriages, family conflict, car problems, death, depression, anxiety, etc. can blind us.

Or you may have a vocation in the religious life, or are a single lay person, which comes with its own set of challenges.

If you are reading this you probably have: a place to live, food, transportation, and family/friends that care about you.

Those things are important but they are only temporal. Most of all let us be thankful for our Catholic Faith.

If you are reading these words you probably are able to practice your faith free from persecution.

Thank God for your access to the Sacraments. Thank God for the small things you encounter each day.

God Bless You!

How to use this journal...

Each daily journal page consists of writing down what you are thankful for, duh! But just as important an area to express **why** you are thankful.

At the bottom there is a place to jot down people to pray for. This can be family and friends , of course, but also think about government leaders, the Pope, bishops, and priests. Or, pray for someone who has wronged you in the past.

There are four "prompt" pages throughout to help with reflection.

Thankful to be Catholic

Thanks Be to God for: **Date:**

_____

_____

_____

_____

_____

_____

Why I am Thankful:

_____

_____

_____

_____

_____

People to Pray for:

_____

_____

_____

_____

Thankful to be Catholic

Thanks Be to God for: **Date:**

_____

_____

_____

_____

_____

Why I am Thankful:

_____

_____

_____

_____

_____

People to Pray for:

_____

_____

_____

_____

Thankful to be Catholic

Thanks Be to God for: **Date:**

_____

_____

_____

_____

_____

Why I am Thankful:

_____

_____

_____

_____

_____

People to Pray for:

_____

_____

_____

_____

Thankful to be Catholic

Thanks Be to God for: **Date:**

_____

_____

_____

_____

_____

Why I am Thankful:

_____

_____

_____

_____

People to Pray for:

_____

_____

_____

_____

Thankful to be Catholic

Thanks Be to God for: **Date:**

_____

_____

_____

_____

_____

Why I am Thankful:

_____

_____

_____

_____

People to Pray for:

_____

_____

_____

_____

Thankful to be Catholic

Thanks Be to God for: **Date:**

_____

_____

_____

_____

_____

Why I am Thankful:

_____

_____

_____

_____

_____

People to Pray for:

_____

_____

_____

_____

Thankful to be Catholic

Thanks Be to God for: **Date:**

_____

_____

_____

_____

_____

_____

Why I am Thankful:

_____

_____

_____

_____

_____

People to Pray for:

_____

_____

_____

_____

Thankful to be Catholic

Thanks Be to God for:

Date:

_____

_____

_____

_____

_____

Why I am Thankful:

_____

_____

_____

_____

People to Pray for:

_____

_____

_____

_____

Thankful to be Catholic

Thanks Be to God for: **Date:**

_____

_____

_____

_____

_____

Why I am Thankful:

_____

_____

_____

_____

People to Pray for:

_____

_____

_____

Thankful to be Catholic

Thanks Be to God for: **Date:**

_____

_____

_____

_____

_____

Why I am Thankful:

_____

_____

_____

_____

People to Pray for:

_____

_____

_____

_____

Thankful to be Catholic

Thanks Be to God for:

Date:

_____

_____

_____

_____

_____

Why I am Thankful:

_____

_____

_____

_____

_____

People to Pray for:

_____

_____

_____

_____

Thankful to be Catholic

Thanks Be to God for: **Date:**

_____

_____

_____

_____

_____

Why I am Thankful:

_____

_____

_____

_____

People to Pray for:

_____

_____

_____

_____

Thankful to be Catholic

Thanks Be to God for: **Date:**

_____

_____

_____

_____

_____

Why I am Thankful:

_____

_____

_____

_____

_____

People to Pray for:

_____

_____

_____

_____

Thankful to be Catholic

Thanks Be to God for: Date:

_____

_____

_____

_____

_____

Why I am Thankful:

_____

_____

_____

_____

People to Pray for:

_____

_____

_____

_____

Thankful to be Catholic

Thanks Be to God for: **Date:**

_____

_____

_____

_____

_____

Why I am Thankful:

_____

_____

_____

_____

People to Pray for:

_____

_____

_____

Thankful to be Catholic

Thanks Be to God for: **Date:**

_____

_____

_____

_____

_____

Why I am Thankful:

_____

_____

_____

_____

People to Pray for:

_____

_____

_____

_____

Thankful to be Catholic

Thanks Be to God for: **Date:**

_____

_____

_____

_____

_____

_____

Why I am Thankful:

_____

_____

_____

_____

_____

People to Pray for:

_____

_____

_____

_____

Thankful to be Catholic

Thanks Be to God for: **Date:**

_____

_____

_____

_____

_____

Why I am Thankful:

_____

_____

_____

_____

People to Pray for:

_____

_____

_____

Thankful to be Catholic

Thanks Be to God for: **Date:**

_____

_____

_____

_____

_____

_____

Why I am Thankful:

_____

_____

_____

_____

_____

People to Pray for:

_____

_____

_____

_____

Thankful to be Catholic

Thanks Be to God for: **Date:**

_____

_____

_____

_____

_____

_____

Why I am Thankful:

_____

_____

_____

_____

_____

People to Pray for:

_____

_____

_____

_____

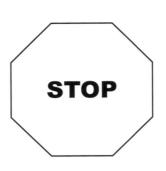

STOP

In a world of negativity, it's easy to overlook blessings in our life. Here are a couple of ideas to help you along.

A great...

Meal I've had recently:

_____

Place I've been:

_____

Friend who just listens:

_____

Sermon I've heard:

_____

Book I've read:

_____

"I give thee thanks, O Lord, with my whole heart..."
- Psalm 138:1

Thankful for My Faith

Thanks Be to God for: **Date:**

_____

_____

_____

_____

_____

Why I am Thankful:

_____

_____

_____

_____

_____

People to Pray for:

_____

_____

_____

_____

Thankful for My Faith

Thanks Be to God for: **Date:**

_____

_____

_____

_____

_____

_____

Why I am Thankful:

_____

_____

_____

_____

_____

People to Pray for:

_____

_____

_____

_____

Thankful for My Faith

Thanks Be to God for: **Date:**

_____

_____

_____

_____

_____

_____

Why I am Thankful:

_____

_____

_____

_____

_____

People to Pray for:

_____

_____

_____

_____

Thankful for My Faith

Thanks Be to God for: **Date:**

_____

_____

_____

_____

_____

Why I am Thankful:

_____

_____

_____

_____

People to Pray for:

_____

_____

_____

_____

Thankful for My Faith

Thanks Be to God for: **Date:**

_____

_____

_____

_____

_____

Why I am Thankful:

_____

_____

_____

_____

_____

People to Pray for:

_____

_____

_____

_____

Thankful for My Faith

Thanks Be to God for: **Date:**

_____

_____

_____

_____

_____

_____

Why I am Thankful:

_____

_____

_____

_____

_____

People to Pray for:

_____

_____

_____

_____

Thankful for My Faith

Thanks Be to God for:

Date:

_____

_____

_____

_____

_____

_____

Why I am Thankful:

_____

_____

_____

_____

_____

People to Pray for:

_____

_____

_____

_____

Thankful for My Faith

Thanks Be to God for: **Date:**

_____

_____

_____

_____

_____

_____

Why I am Thankful:

_____

_____

_____

_____

_____

People to Pray for:

_____

_____

_____

_____

Thankful for My Faith

Thanks Be to God for: **Date:**

_____

_____

_____

_____

_____

Why I am Thankful:

_____

_____

_____

_____

People to Pray for:

_____

_____

_____

_____

Thankful for My Faith

Thanks Be to God for: **Date:**

_____

_____

_____

_____

_____

_____

Why I am Thankful:

_____

_____

_____

_____

_____

People to Pray for:

_____

_____

_____

_____

Thankful for My Faith

Thanks Be to God for: Date:

_____

_____

_____

_____

_____

_____

Why I am Thankful:

_____

_____

_____

_____

_____

People to Pray for:

_____

_____

_____

_____

Thankful for My Faith

Thanks Be to God for: **Date:**

_____

_____

_____

_____

_____

Why I am Thankful:

_____

_____

_____

_____

_____

People to Pray for:

_____

_____

_____

_____

Thankful for My Faith

Thanks Be to God for: Date:

_____

_____

_____

_____

_____

_____

Why I am Thankful:

_____

_____

_____

_____

_____

People to Pray for:

_____

_____

_____

_____

Thankful for My Faith

Thanks Be to God for: **Date:**

_____

_____

_____

_____

_____

_____

Why I am Thankful:

_____

_____

_____

_____

_____

People to Pray for:

_____

_____

_____

_____

Thankful for My Faith

Thanks Be to God for: **Date:**

_____

_____

_____

_____

_____

Why I am Thankful:

_____

_____

_____

_____

People to Pray for:

_____

_____

_____

_____

Thankful for My Faith

Thanks Be to God for: Date:

_____

_____

_____

_____

_____

Why I am Thankful:

_____

_____

_____

_____

People to Pray for:

_____

_____

_____

Thankful for My Faith

Thanks Be to God for: **Date:**

_____

_____

_____

_____

_____

Why I am Thankful:

_____

_____

_____

_____

_____

People to Pray for:

_____

_____

_____

_____

Thankful for My Faith

Thanks Be to God for: **Date:**

_____

_____

_____

_____

_____

Why I am Thankful:

_____

_____

_____

_____

People to Pray for:

_____

_____

_____

_____

Thankful for My Faith

Thanks Be to God for: **Date:**

_____

_____

_____

_____

_____

Why I am Thankful:

_____

_____

_____

_____

People to Pray for:

_____

_____

_____

_____

Thankful for My Faith

Thanks Be to God for: **Date:**

_____

_____

_____

_____

_____

Why I am Thankful:

_____

_____

_____

_____

_____

People to Pray for:

_____

_____

_____

_____

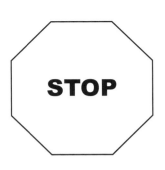

STOP

Somedays it's tough to remember the good things in life. Sometimes our prayer life can seem dry. Here are some questions to ask yourself:

Do I pray the Rosary regularly?

Do I examine my conscience at the end of the day?

How much spiritual reading am I doing?

Jot down a couple of things you can improve upon to help you focus on the good around you.

_____

_____

_____

_____

"Thank God ahead of time." – Bl. Solanus Casey

Thankful for My Loved Ones

Thanks Be to God for: Date:

_____

_____

_____

_____

_____

Why I am Thankful:

_____

_____

_____

_____

People to Pray for:

_____

_____

_____

Thankful for My Loved Ones

Thanks Be to God for: Date:

_____

_____

_____

_____

_____

Why I am Thankful:

_____

_____

_____

_____

_____

People to Pray for:

_____

_____

_____

_____

Thankful for My Loved Ones

Thanks Be to God for: Date:

_____

_____

_____

_____

_____

Why I am Thankful:

_____

_____

_____

_____

People to Pray for:

_____

_____

_____

_____

Thankful for My Loved Ones

Thanks Be to God for: Date:

_____

_____

_____

_____

_____

_____

Why I am Thankful:

_____

_____

_____

_____

_____

People to Pray for:

_____

_____

_____

_____

Thankful for My Loved Ones

Thanks Be to God for: **Date:**

_____

_____

_____

_____

_____

Why I am Thankful:

_____

_____

_____

_____

_____

People to Pray for:

_____

_____

_____

_____

Thankful for My Loved Ones

Thanks Be to God for:

Date:

_____

_____

_____

_____

_____

_____

Why I am Thankful:

_____

_____

_____

_____

_____

People to Pray for:

_____

_____

_____

_____

Thankful for My Loved Ones

Thanks Be to God for: Date:

_____

_____

_____

_____

_____

Why I am Thankful:

_____

_____

_____

_____

People to Pray for:

_____

_____

_____

Thankful for My Loved Ones

Thanks Be to God for: **Date:**

_____

_____

_____

_____

_____

Why I am Thankful:

_____

_____

_____

_____

People to Pray for:

_____

_____

_____

_____

Thankful for My Loved Ones

Thanks Be to God for: **Date:**

_____

_____

_____

_____

_____

Why I am Thankful:

_____

_____

_____

_____

_____

People to Pray for:

_____

_____

_____

_____

Thankful for My Loved Ones

Thanks Be to God for: **Date:**

_____

_____

_____

_____

_____

_____

Why I am Thankful:

_____

_____

_____

_____

_____

People to Pray for:

_____

_____

_____

_____

Thankful for My Loved Ones

Thanks Be to God for: **Date:**

_____

_____

_____

_____

_____

_____

Why I am Thankful:

_____

_____

_____

_____

People to Pray for:

_____

_____

_____

_____

Thankful for My Loved Ones

Thanks Be to God for: **Date:**

_____

_____

_____

_____

_____

_____

Why I am Thankful:

_____

_____

_____

_____

_____

People to Pray for:

_____

_____

_____

_____

Thankful for My Loved Ones

Thanks Be to God for: **Date:**

_____

_____

_____

_____

_____

Why I am Thankful:

_____

_____

_____

_____

People to Pray for:

_____

_____

_____

_____

Thankful for My Loved Ones

Thanks Be to God for: Date:

_____

_____

_____

_____

_____

Why I am Thankful:

_____

_____

_____

_____

_____

People to Pray for:

_____

_____

_____

_____

Thankful for My Loved Ones

Thanks Be to God for: **Date:**

_____

_____

_____

_____

_____

_____

Why I am Thankful:

_____

_____

_____

_____

_____

People to Pray for:

_____

_____

_____

_____

Thankful for My Loved Ones

Thanks Be to God for: Date:

_____

_____

_____

_____

_____

_____

Why I am Thankful:

_____

_____

_____

_____

_____

People to Pray for:

_____

_____

_____

_____

Thankful for My Loved Ones

Thanks Be to God for: Date:

_____

_____

_____

_____

_____

Why I am Thankful:

_____

_____

_____

_____

People to Pray for:

_____

_____

_____

_____

Thankful for My Loved Ones

Thanks Be to God for: **Date:**

_____

_____

_____

_____

_____

_____

Why I am Thankful:

_____

_____

_____

_____

_____

People to Pray for:

_____

_____

_____

_____

Thankful for My Loved Ones

Thanks Be to God for: Date:

_____

_____

_____

_____

_____

_____

Why I am Thankful:

_____

_____

_____

_____

_____

People to Pray for:

_____

_____

_____

_____

Thankful for My Loved Ones

Thanks Be to God for: **Date:**

_____

_____

_____

_____

_____

_____

Why I am Thankful:

_____

_____

_____

_____

_____

People to Pray for:

_____

_____

_____

_____

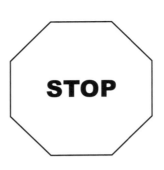

STOP

God always answers our prayers, however sometimes the answer is "no." Other times God will give us what we are asking for, even if it's not in the exact way we think is best.

Write down some of your recent prayers where God has answered them with some kind of a "yes."

_____

_____

_____

_____

_____

"He who prays most, receives most." –St. Alphonsus Liguori

Thankful for the Sacraments

Thanks Be to God for: Date:

_____

_____

_____

_____

_____

_____

Why I am Thankful:

_____

_____

_____

_____

_____

People to Pray for:

_____

_____

_____

_____

Thankful for the Sacraments

Thanks Be to God for: **Date:**

_____

_____

_____

_____

_____

_____

Why I am Thankful:

_____

_____

_____

_____

_____

People to Pray for:

_____

_____

_____

_____

Thankful for the Sacraments

Thanks Be to God for: **Date:**

_____

_____

_____

_____

_____

Why I am Thankful:

_____

_____

_____

_____

_____

People to Pray for:

_____

_____

_____

_____

Thankful for the Sacraments

Thanks Be to God for: **Date:**

_____

_____

_____

_____

_____

_____

Why I am Thankful:

_____

_____

_____

_____

_____

People to Pray for:

_____

_____

_____

_____

Thankful for the Sacraments

Thanks Be to God for: **Date:**

_____

_____

_____

_____

_____

_____

Why I am Thankful:

_____

_____

_____

_____

_____

People to Pray for:

_____

_____

_____

_____

Thankful for the Sacraments

Thanks Be to God for: **Date:**

_____

_____

_____

_____

_____

_____

Why I am Thankful:

_____

_____

_____

_____

People to Pray for:

_____

_____

_____

_____

Thankful for the Sacraments

Thanks Be to God for: **Date:**

_____

_____

_____

_____

_____

_____

Why I am Thankful:

_____

_____

_____

_____

_____

People to Pray for:

_____

_____

_____

_____

Thankful for the Sacraments

Thanks Be to God for: *Date:*

_____

_____

_____

_____

_____

_____

Why I am Thankful:

_____

_____

_____

_____

_____

People to Pray for:

_____

_____

_____

_____

Thankful for the Sacraments

Thanks Be to God for: **Date:**

_____

_____

_____

_____

_____

_____

Why I am Thankful:

_____

_____

_____

_____

_____

People to Pray for:

_____

_____

_____

_____

Thankful for the Sacraments

Thanks Be to God for: **Date:**

_____

_____

_____

_____

_____

_____

Why I am Thankful:

_____

_____

_____

_____

People to Pray for:

_____

_____

_____

_____

Thankful for the Sacraments

Thanks Be to God for: *Date:*

_____

_____

_____

_____

_____

Why I am Thankful:

_____

_____

_____

_____

_____

People to Pray for:

_____

_____

_____

_____

Thankful for the Sacraments

Thanks Be to God for: **Date:**

_____

_____

_____

_____

_____

_____

Why I am Thankful:

_____

_____

_____

_____

_____

People to Pray for:

_____

_____

_____

_____

Thankful for the Sacraments

Thanks Be to God for: *Date:*

_____

_____

_____

_____

_____

Why I am Thankful:

_____

_____

_____

_____

People to Pray for:

_____

_____

_____

_____

Thankful for the Sacraments

Thanks Be to God for: Date:

_____

_____

_____

_____

_____

_____

Why I am Thankful:

_____

_____

_____

_____

_____

People to Pray for:

_____

_____

_____

_____

Thankful for the Sacraments

Thanks Be to God for: *Date:*

_____

_____

_____

_____

_____

_____

Why I am Thankful:

_____

_____

_____

_____

_____

People to Pray for:

_____

_____

_____

_____

Thankful for the Sacraments

Thanks Be to God for: **Date:**

_____

_____

_____

_____

_____

_____

Why I am Thankful:

_____

_____

_____

_____

_____

People to Pray for:

_____

_____

_____

_____

Thankful for the Sacraments

Thanks Be to God for: *Date:*

_____

_____

_____

_____

_____

_____

Why I am Thankful:

_____

_____

_____

_____

_____

People to Pray for:

_____

_____

_____

_____

Thankful for the Sacraments

Thanks Be to God for: **Date:**

_____

_____

_____

_____

_____

_____

Why I am Thankful:

_____

_____

_____

_____

_____

People to Pray for:

_____

_____

_____

_____

Thankful for the Sacraments

Thanks Be to God for: **Date:**

_____

_____

_____

_____

_____

Why I am Thankful:

_____

_____

_____

_____

People to Pray for:

_____

_____

_____

_____

Thankful for the Sacraments

Thanks Be to God for: **Date:**

_____

_____

_____

_____

_____

_____

Why I am Thankful:

_____

_____

_____

_____

_____

People to Pray for:

_____

_____

_____

_____

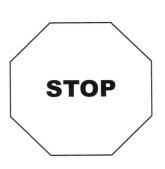

As Catholics we know that God allows bad things to happen as he will not interfere with our free will.

However, God can and does make good come out of evil. Jot down some times where something good came out of what seemed to be a bad situation.

_____

_____

_____

_____

_____

"God judged it better to bring good out of evil than to suffer no evil to exist." – St. Augustine

Thankful for Graces Received

Thanks Be to God for: **Date:**

_____

_____

_____

_____

_____

_____

Why I am Thankful:

_____

_____

_____

_____

_____

People to Pray for:

_____

_____

_____

_____

Thankful for Graces Received

Thanks Be to God for: Date:

_____

_____

_____

_____

_____

Why I am Thankful:
_____

_____

_____

_____

People to Pray for:
_____

_____

_____

_____

Thankful for Graces Received

Thanks Be to God for: **Date:**

_____

_____

_____

_____

_____

_____

Why I am Thankful:

_____

_____

_____

_____

_____

People to Pray for:

_____

_____

_____

_____

Thankful for Graces Received

Thanks Be to God for: **Date:**

_____

_____

_____

_____

_____

Why I am Thankful:

_____

_____

_____

_____

People to Pray for:

_____

_____

_____

_____

Thankful for Graces Received

Thanks Be to God for: *Date:*

_____

_____

_____

_____

_____

_____

Why I am Thankful:

_____

_____

_____

_____

_____

People to Pray for:

_____

_____

_____

_____

Thankful for Graces Received

Thanks Be to God for: **Date:**

_____

_____

_____

_____

_____

_____

Why I am Thankful:

_____

_____

_____

_____

_____

People to Pray for:

_____

_____

_____

_____

Thankful for Graces Received

Thanks Be to God for: *Date:*

_____

_____

_____

_____

_____

_____

Why I am Thankful:

_____

_____

_____

_____

_____

People to Pray for:

_____

_____

_____

_____

Thankful for Graces Received

Thanks Be to God for: **Date:**

_____

_____

_____

_____

_____

_____

Why I am Thankful:

_____

_____

_____

_____

_____

People to Pray for:

_____

_____

_____

_____

Thankful for Graces Received

Thanks Be to God for: Date:

_____

_____

_____

_____

_____

_____

Why I am Thankful:

_____

_____

_____

_____

_____

People to Pray for:

_____

_____

_____

_____

Thankful for Graces Received

Thanks Be to God for: Date:

_____

_____

_____

_____

_____

Why I am Thankful:

_____

_____

_____

_____

People to Pray for:

_____

_____

_____

_____

Thankful for Graces Received

Thanks Be to God for: **Date:**

_____

_____

_____

_____

_____

_____

Why I am Thankful:

_____

_____

_____

_____

_____

People to Pray for:

_____

_____

_____

_____

Thankful for Graces Received

Thanks Be to God for: **Date:**

_____

_____

_____

_____

_____

_____

Why I am Thankful:

_____

_____

_____

_____

_____

People to Pray for:

_____

_____

_____

_____

Thankful for Graces Received

Thanks Be to God for: *Date:*

_____

_____

_____

_____

_____

_____

Why I am Thankful:

_____

_____

_____

_____

_____

People to Pray for:

_____

_____

_____

_____

Thankful for Graces Received

Thanks Be to God for: Date:

_____

_____

_____

_____

_____

_____

Why I am Thankful:

_____

_____

_____

_____

_____

People to Pray for:

_____

_____

_____

_____

Thankful for Graces Received

Thanks Be to God for: **Date:**

_____

_____

_____

_____

_____

_____

Why I am Thankful:

_____

_____

_____

_____

_____

People to Pray for:

_____

_____

_____

_____

Thankful for Graces Received

Thanks Be to God for: **Date:**

_____

_____

_____

_____

_____

Why I am Thankful:

_____

_____

_____

_____

_____

People to Pray for:

_____

_____

_____

Thankful for Graces Received

Thanks Be to God for: **Date:**

_____

_____

_____

_____

_____

_____

Why I am Thankful:

_____

_____

_____

_____

_____

People to Pray for:

_____

_____

_____

_____

Thankful for Graces Received

Thanks Be to God for: **Date:**

_____

_____

_____

_____

_____

Why I am Thankful:

_____

_____

_____

_____

_____

People to Pray for:

_____

_____

_____

_____

Thankful for Graces Received

Thanks Be to God for: *Date:*

_____

_____

_____

_____

_____

_____

Why I am Thankful:

_____

_____

_____

_____

_____

People to Pray for:

_____

_____

_____

_____

Thankful for Graces Received

Thanks Be to God for: **Date:**

_____

_____

_____

_____

_____

Why I am Thankful:

_____

_____

_____

_____

People to Pray for:

_____

_____

_____

_____

doodle page

doodle page

Thank you for purchasing this Catholic journal. We hope you found value in this gratitude journal. Check out our other Catholic books like our popular planners.

God Bless!

Made in the USA
Middletown, DE
22 November 2020